Bathing in the River of Ashes

Western Literature Series

Bathing in the River of Ashes

Poems

Shaun T. Griffin

 University of Nevada Press *Reno Las Vegas*

Western Literature Series

University of Nevada Press, Reno, Nevada 89557 USA
Copyright © 1989, 1991, 1992, 1994, 1995, 1996, 1999
by Shaun T. Griffin
All rights reserved
Manufactured in the United States of America
Cover design by Kristina E. Kachele

Library of Congress Cataloging-in-Publication Data
Griffin, Shaun T. (Shaun Timothy), 1953–
    Bathing in the river of ashes : poems / Shaun T. Griffin.
      p. cm. —(Western literature series)
    ISBN 0-87417-331-0 (pbk. : alk. paper)
    I. Title. II. Series.
    PS3557.R489127B38   1999
    811'.54 —dc21   98-37175
                                       CIP

The paper used in this book meets the requirements of
American National Standard for Information Sciences—
Permanence of Paper for Printed Library Materials, ANSI
Z39.48–1984. Binding materials were selected for strength
and durability.

First Printing

08 07 06 05 04 03 02 01 00 99 5 4 3 2 1

For my father
whose hands I feel still
and mother
who shapes the hands to come

I have a pact of love with beauty;
I have a pact of blood with my people.
—Pablo Neruda

Contents

Nevada No Longer

October in Battle Mountain

for Rafael and Ana

In a town so small a train
clogs the lone passage east
with its bump of coal, flat cars, and
machinery blackened for war,
they wait in a Chevy truck
for the nod of the semaphore: a moment
stopped on tracks, the veins that feed
the mines, the livestock, and the weathered
patios of October. A displaced Texan
clutches the fish-and-game guide:

"Opening day—I'll be gone at six—
chukar'll run you into the ground."

And still the whistle blows, back
from the throated diesel, plumes
dark as memory in the high desert wind.
Cottonwoods clatter their orange reeds;
his son kicks the leaves like strangely devalued
    pesos.
Inside, she folds salt and onions in the mortar.
Fall has almost stripped this town of green.
In two short months the whistle will signal death:
a cold white sun will poke shapes dry in the ice;
a dog's wail at daylight, hard against the glass,

and tightened in a knot on the horizon,
a train, clipping its way through sleep.

After Lunch at the Blueberry Cafe:
Las Vegas, 1994

for Stephen Shu-Ning Liu

Soon the Strip will flame
with neon, and no tourist
will return as he came
to the aboriginal soil
that crowds to dust where

patio lawns and weathered
magpies spar for water
or any ghost of moisture
in the momentary desert
this late spring day.

At the substation I finger
Walter Clark's trembling leaves
and wonder what rogue seed
choked to birth them
on this six-lane highway.

But I cannot walk this sand like a city,
only the wells of sadness
that lie in pockets of overturned sky
and the few wild things left
to mark my journey south—yellow flowers

pitchforked with ants
on a creosote bush. Whose home
this dusted prairie we paved
for pleasure? Whose home
do we squirrel away to now?

Hawthorne

for Gary Short

In a town where bombs
buy a day's work and bunkers
blight the desert like bones,
how happy can you be
straddling a stool at El Capitán
with the windows coiled in smoke
and the jukebox jarring K-9
through the reeds of country soul?

The casino fades to lavender
shoulders on Highway 95.
Tourists brake to read "Danger—
Low Flying Aircraft, Do Not Stop,"
and the hangars climb to the sky
and detours swallow transport trucks
bound for Reno or beyond.

And still the bunkers lie, mouths open
like barrels in the rain.

The Cliff House Saloon, quiet as fog,
boasts "Armed Forces Day—
Proud to Serve You," and the old ones
wait for the second Tuesday in July
when the hydroplanes
light up Walker Lake.
Even it looks flatter than it should.

The children play on decommissioned
three-inch, fifty-caliber anti-aircraft guns
as if they were powder-blue
dinosaurs in Ladybird Park,
thinking, how much better can it get?
In a once-mighty high school,
seniors graduate to thieve from Mormon sky.

And bunkers die in peacetime.

The barracks are nearly closed now.
The moon rises in sills of solitude
and the last drunk shuffles from
Joe's Tavern like a cloud
come to rescue this swollen town.
And the wind moves like a skirt
through the clapboard siding
beached in stones at her feet.

The Meyer Cabin, Jarbidge

What holy thread made man come down this road?
To this sovereign stable, chinked with mud,
animal fat, and barrel staves,
a stream-fed backwoods cabin high
in the wedge of wilderness the first
federal survey team cut from Nevada, sloped
to nearly forty acres, and if you include the
    Diamond A,
broken as it is from the world, island after island
of land atop the river gorges, it may as well be
another country, out here in the vacant
West old Abbey bore, bookless, looking

for a hand, and he knew then the song
was wild and migratory like birds,
coming here dusted as planks, peeled
from the road of forty-seven miles in, good God
was it Jarbidge held in the black wake of fire
summer last, and storm-sweet Monday in July,
unpredictable pee-pot, cantankerous valley,
have I finally wept this womb of cold earth
and left it to seethe in the bedspring air
some tall cloudless day in a crooked house come
    down
to fiddle our lives in this small fork of creation?

At the Old Santa Fe Club in Goldfield

The Sundog Bed and Breakfast sign
squeaks like an iron saddle in the wind.
Even the diesels downshifting at the curve
slowly fade. Gravel rings the schoolyard
in a rosary for better times, and kids climb the
     poles
that anchor double-wides to the ground.

"Gold went down and they say the Test Site is
     going
to New Mexico in '91. Bad management, I guess."

Out here, rumors and books, like all quiet things,
blow through the cracks of moon and sun
where people sit thankful for their coming.

                    "You serve food?" I ask.

"No, not much here since the mine closed.
Be like everything else, I guess—
they'll wait till there's a foot-a-snow and it's colder
'n-a-bear's ass to open it again. The Mozart Club
is the only one serving food anymore."

Game One of the World Series tonight.
She tilts the ash from her cigarette and says,
"Land's going down, like everything else, I guess."

If the Greyhound stops at all, it will be
the driver who steps off for coffee, or Don's Donuts
trucked in from Tonopah. Later, at the Gables,
there's crazy chatter in the cellar,
shadows growing on the family plot, and
nothing but rust to take them from here.

Tumbleweeds and Toenails:
Weed Abatement in Silver Springs

Out here on the carrion highway
three men, two semis and a propane
torch to kill the devil weed,
the only vegetation
on this black stretch that hooks
Mule Flats to Leeteville Junction.

In one more month the weeds will blow away,
and by Christmas, snow will light
their tails at first sun. Were it not
for the occasional mask of motion
I'd drive to Austin before seeing
the orange men move.

But why turn back skeletons
with their tools? Is it that rain
simply won't do or the frenzy
of fired gun at so wicked a thistle?
Either way, they pour it on, as if at play.
Highway 50 will never be bordered again.

Nevada No Longer

This is a case in which the public
has to trust the scientists.
—Tony Buono, USGS Hydrologist,
Nevada Test Site

Nevada is never on the map, not now,
not ever.
      If only
I could finger a word
for the few who live
          by the sun,
what would it be: itinerant,
sparse dragon people
          who fly
in the sand and spin before the books
that name a cactus to clothe
the loins of uranium down deep?

No, it would not be harsh; rather
we live here.
We raise family, split wood,
shovel snow, and read of our absence.

Nevada is never on the map,
not now, not ever,
          save the day
a green lung percolates
from two miles below volcanic tuff—
then you will recognize us
as the place that kills

or was killed, but for now
I cannot find a way down Alternate 95 —
not scholarly, not radical, not
known. And still, faces cling
to the taverns of Beatty,
Tonopah, and Yerington.

Where do I go to lie with the yucca? California?
No, it is many things but quiet.
Oregon? No, it is wet and
dry there, so I remain
home
with states before and aft
coming like insects
to the Test Site, coming
with something to read.

Today, I tell my son
of a desert with no name. He remarks
"Why?" I do not know—Nevada is
never on the map, not now,
not ever.

On the Death of the Culture Dog, Nevada's Last Bookstore

I pull the solitary handle—not another slot—
and know the smell of something fine
gathered for posterity: William Everson's poems
the fifth of fifty, signed, handmade by Capra Press.
A final volume of recollections by Miller,
and further still, Shakespeare aging
in a china cabinet. Somewhere in the lost
temple of the desert, these few have made a
forest, book-like, of belief in things rare
and old. Belief that cannot be copied:
a remarkable feat where tourists play
in the change girl's hand. Even the paint
on the building is the color of
                    sand at sunset.

The message comes in bold letters: *40% OFF!*
Going out of business June 12—and
turn to take my swipes at a shelf.
Whom will it be this fertile time?
Merwin, Paz, Bishop, or Wright—
I cannot take them all. No
money will buy these friends. They will
return to Bronx warehouses and bitter the columns
of bean-counters in high-rise offices. Good
for them, I think, let the bastards burn
                    poetry for heat in Manhattan.

But we live in the desert,
somehow richer for a stretch of sun.
We will carry on without literature for trade
but not like it. Come back, Culture Dog,
we are churchless with your leaving. There is no
   place
to footnote a loss in the bookstore granaries
               of America.

The New Western Prairie

The Sparks cowboys ride the early prairie:
diesel cabs twist the downtown music
of pigeons and porcine tourists tipping
change buckets from the Nugget.

The unknown faces slip from ware-
house windows until darkness returns
and Jack's Coffee Shop idles a crew to work,
past the tire store, the car lots dressed in pastels

for summer and all the world is on B Street
born again by businessmen somehow lost
on the new western prairie. Even the
scented cowgirl pleads innocence

and she decides blinking by, this part of town
is better left to die. This is the merry-go-round
she refuses to ride.

First Cast, Late December, Pyramid Lake

for Jess Hayashi, 1951–1991

Today, fly-fishing the algaled dark
of Pyramid, snowstorm at my back,
I heard you in the mud hens, crying

when the cutthroat snapped the leader,
pink mouth opened to saline water,
it was you who swallowed,

bore the wooly worm in your maw,
my gloved forefinger pressed to cork
and the fluorescent line stiff in silver tow.

We floated the silted bed, squirmed
the Pleistocene floor, then calm in waders
you mocked California gulls from the nets,

plunged coots in the tufa. "Worthless bird,"
you said on our last visit with full, steamed
breath, then swore stalking in the wind,

ladder lapping the shore. Brittle man,
I can never catch the friend you were,
but I will fish to the end.

And when my rod buckles,
I will know it is you who bites
and boldly spins the reel at my palm.

Magpie Funeral

My scavenger husband picked you
from pavement, drove the eight miles
up the grade, found a telephone spool
off the porch, and waited for flesh to dry.

Black-billed to scruff the desert,
he wanted you for the alligator headdress
on his flatbed Chevy. But when the breath
of twenty birds came solemn from the locusts,
we knew it was more than carrion on the circular
    table.

Robed in black and white, they swooped
one at a time to the wooden altar.
For over an hour, their hushed flight
echoed the loss of a crow dancer
with the last dry speech of family.

Each bird, dressed in shadow, came
without calling, without invitation,
touched kin to understand:
scavenger, you can eat no more.

Never satiated, they flew to scour
what little breath had settled
in the hollow of your craving,
leaving you with wings spread,
oh bird of prey, as if to reach sky.

Geiger Grade

for a child gone wild to the road

There are many deaths at elevation 6,789
born of hesitation
    drought
    or flight

and I name them
    gray squirrel
    cheat grass
    black gnat

but I cannot name you
    child of the silver car
careening over the mountain
    on senior ditch day.

And when I ride a bicycle
    up this highway
to find the skid marks
    that laid you bare

the footprints to a headstone
    of blue sunglasses
    chrome body trim
    angled to hands

    the female safety buckle
    opened to sky
    and ashless tray

the whole of you pitched
      on a hillside of igneous rock
I remember the scant tissue
      on which we lay our lives.

Left to be consoled
      by the birth of a flower
yellow and nameless
      I coast the grade home,

a blackbird teetering on the wind.

Those People

Tetherball

The merry-go-round in their front yard
has no horses,
it sits still by night and after school
they shimmy steel, tie the knot, and swat till they
   bleed.
Boys, all of them,
and a girl
at the corner of East 8th and Morrill
and the landlord puckers for rent,
the wrecker
tows father's car to the bank.
The last dandelion slides to the ground.
They squirt
the slang of street tag,
swing like cats from the post,
and mother will ask if she played
tetherball
when she goes home to pluck
from a nest of bottles
her favorite glass
for milk.

They Go Gathering Pine Nuts

Out there on the grade,
brittle as a couple of rain gutters
they stoop to misbehave: cussing
cantankerous, stuck in the craw of cones,
it's nearly a holiday from the wifely
flatulence of home, festering with sap
Buddy and Hal, they grumble in suspenders:

"They're too damn small—"

        "They're what we get—"

gristly like an old married couple
they toss the broken ones to the ground.
A Paiute ghost slows a breath of wind
and still they burst with thumbs,
bootlegged and haggard, to strip the piñon.
Saddled in sun at midday, caught
between needle and stone, they knock shins

to tailgate and paddle through the ugly
tales that collar round their mountain
before the growling stiffness sets in and
they retrieve the burlap bags to slide
the Dodge to town, boil and dry
the wooden shells that yearly drop
to feed the restless boys again.

First and Last Things

for C., on being released from prison

The sun rose to part steel. Today
you stepped from that place
where they kept you cold and dark
as anthracite coal, walked twenty feet
from the yard that burns men down
and gave your last goodbye to

    the aluminum tray they fed you on
    the photo with number pigeoned below
    the blue cotton sweat gathered under your
       arms
    the six A.M. count cleared before you,

frozen in the rails of feeling, walked not
ten feet to hear the bars barrel
down to the scratch of hoes on the warden's lawn.

And though it was your last day
you managed to look back and befriend
a face full of memories so bleak
even your eyes could not hold them.

Then, like a cloud breaking,
you
    stepped through the gate of our house
and for the first time in eleven-and-a-half years

climbed stairs, sniffed blue spruce
ran fingers through golden retriever
touched sparkling cider to tongue
crossed asphalt laid for all to travel
breathed sky and bore no sadness

when you saw sixty miles of mountain
and valley and said, "I want you
to write this down: *Now those years
are gone to dreams.*" My son ran
balloons through your arms
and you burst into color
like the fingers of crocus at your feet.

Then you ate, for the first time,
breakfast on legs of maple and hand-painted plates
so pink and yellow I think you gave up eating
    altogether
and sat shining before the cactus given you
for the journey home.

La Desterrada

for Emma Sepúlveda

Woman without soil,
you carve roots
from the stones of this town
and wander, if ever you can,
among the cowboys, call girls, and
neon of the North.

So many faces
held in your hands:
you quilt the fabric
of their lives
in black and white,
silence that must be sung.

Child of Chile,
you left the fear of hiding
and now, two decades gone,
you long to close
the dream of life in a land
without exile.

Melancholy believer,
come finish the dark
days of your youth,
on this snow-capped
stone place
of our meeting.

Un moreno en la cocina

no tiene ojos
ni manos
solo una cara
que lleva platos al horno
hasta un lugar cerca de los tenedores
y regresa para nadar
entre las ollas. No conoce
los que comen afuera
los que limpian sus labios
bajo las cucharas y cuchillas
y salen por la puerta
con las manos derechas. Todo el mundo
come así: sin razón
antes del día para salir
cuando el sol baja en los ojos
del moreno que lava los vasos
sobre la memoria de la familia caen
de maíz, de coyote, desde
                el ferrocarril
subiendo la cocina de piedra hasta la casa.

A Brown Man in the Kitchen

has no eyes
nor hands,
only a face
that brings plates to the oven
to a place close to the forks
and returns to swim
among the pots. He does not know
those who eat outside,
those who clean their lips
on spoons and knives
and leave for the door
with right hands. All the world
eats like this: without reason
before the day to leave
when the sun goes down in the eyes
of a brown man who cleans glasses
over the memory of family, fallen
from corn, from coyote, from
                the railroad,
climbing from the stone kitchen of home.

The Border Ink

The child is smoke on the border crossing.
There is no room for her to crawl
the barbed ribbon to sanctuary.
In the land of wagers
to spend the lives of children
the blue rain of uniforms
sails the sand.
She lies with her child
as they circle the sister selves
of dark and thin,
the federal strangers in the endless light of dusk.
It could be tomorrow before she breathes again.
But she will go with them, childless
in her shawl. There will be no face in the tiny
black pool of her eyes. And their report
will drop to a green room of border files.

This Is Not Love's Offering

for a child in the Sudan

Having little to do with Eros
the vulture cranes to feed:
the child of famine recedes
to skin, and the black bird inches
to pierce the web of pulse
playing out on the desert floor.

The bird may not know
the breath of a child, may
be unfamiliar with his sighing.
But soon the two will merge
to prey upon the living
in a photograph.

When the child wakes
to another world, solemn
with the feathers of struggle,
there will be no eyes to receive him,
no camera to record. He will lie
as he was, in the kingdom of birds.

Postscript to Chiapas

I remember the tall river
    that broke with our coming
    to silt the earth with pain.

Absent volition,
    we smote the dirt and ash
    where once the soil stood trees.

My flesh, hours before
    Hiroshima,
    Nagasaki, and

no voice but the torch
    of fascination,
    ether for the fall.

I rode the carriage
    that coiled the enemy,
    a virulent shadow

then braced for the edge
    of our breathing,
    but the sun, miracle of iodine,

came red to remind
    that each small hand must clasp
    the outlaw, agitator, and state.

I bruised the wing of a child,
    found the tassel of hope
    hard at her chest.

And gathered stones to recall
    the mythic ones
    before we came.

The Ring of Chains

When I see two men punch
on the silver screen, and a third bob
like a rabbit between tired strokes
to the torso, men whose heads
snap against the rubber ropes
and shriek in raging sweat
with Budweiser flying
beneath the hands that swing
blood for all to see,

hands with no more room to box
the fields of glass in the city,
hands sewn like barrels to beat
against the screen that beams us live
to the Hacienda Hotel in Las Vegas—

when they stammer to speak the words
to heal such hands as these

there is no canvas on which to fall.

The next day I read of Ali drunk
with Parkinson's and drive through a burn
near Woodfords now two years done—
a mountainside of black Jeffrey, ponderosa.
What have I to give these trees
save the recognition of their sovereign right
to die in a March snowfall?

When I reach the aspen sky of 7,000 feet
the sign reads Hope Valley, Kit Carson Pass.
Soon the warning of clouds
and I flinch the curve—fighting still
                    before the white,
white moon of misery.

"Seems I'm All I've Got Anymore"

She side-stepped the lifeless
flesh of a stroke into the office,
dangled limbs like ice cream,

and managed the words, "I can do this job!"
her voice a sparrow
caught in a fireplace flue.

With no angels to redeem
she begged for a chance
to move in a room of machines.

And they let her perform a function.
Soon the troubled messages flew:
"Who called? I can't read this!"

With her right wrist she scissored manilla
folders on the paper cutter and with her left
worked the halves to the ruler's edge,

having been cut to half-time, her interviews
sliced the long story that trails flesh,
and gathering all the scraps of paper,

she shuffled to the door, mumbling the curious
side effect of living in a full-flesh world:
"I don't know what's going to become of me . . ."

Manumission

Jackson Square, New Orleans

His skin is a sheath for the timid spokes
of passersby. The dark wires of bone
cradle a six-string, muffle voices
that cannot pardon the tone of "Yesterday."
His brow is gathered like ice
on the rim of a glass. He prods the Creole breeze,
as if by incision, to quiet the screams
of dead mothers and fathers before him.

The sweet powdered air dusts the bowl
where nickels pile higher than Grant's Tomb.
A petunia sways in the grass, and the blue notes
burrow on through clouds of painted tourists.
His silver box, though weak, rains the patio
with rhythm, and whether it is stage or hunger
he frets the strings with double fingers—
no one can empty this man of music.

Below sea level, the humid hands
eat from the mouth of the Mississippi.

Madonna in Traffic

Your eyes, shunted away in dark
amniotic fluid, what do you see
staring onto Boulder Highway,
mother straddling the island with cars
slipping either side of her waist,
what face do you look upon
stringing headlight to tail with the
unknown family at the intersection?

Her sign is finger-painted with magenta
letters but you cannot read the words.
Hungry. Pregnant. Need Work. Help Please.
You must not know her ringless stranger
as she coughs the cardboard high into the air
then stills your limbs, swinging into the flesh
you now gather. For seven months
you have trailed jobs to cities hot and broken

and once there, the old streets and soda crackers
came easy but inside the cotton dress
that blows toward Lake Mead, you wonder
if the next exit will find the hot meal
promised in long-ago Kansas, or shots
mother missed hitching out here. This road
has grown like a child and nothing, not traffic,
not plain people will shade the world outside,

but this small face that crowds her skin,
this membrane she touches
with stomach to sign may as well be
her breathing room where it's calm and smooth,
and that's how you feel the fetal drum
looking out on this six-lane highway
with all Las Vegas glowing in the mirror
of every timid glance driving home from work.

Family

Wife is pregnant, will work for food.
The words, black on cardboard, ring
like wooden bells at the McCarran exit.
I-80 is a lonely road, Sparks even more,
and the baby bubbles from her waist
in the morning sun. Beneath the motel sign

they can almost see the tractor-trailer rigs
idle the stop to Sierra Sid's, where *Steak and Eggs*
    for $2.99
blinks in neon and classifieds curl in the sleeper
    cars.
And what phantom brings them to bear
this poor, paved place? The words ring again:
Wife is pregnant, will work for food.

An elegy to the miles, the curious think,
downshifting to the unleavened on the roadside.
America come home to sheet rock and brown
    bread,
but always, in the shadows, their eyes
winnowed from too much travel, speech rote,
spelled with crayons on the way to California,

strung like tangled chimes on the interstate,
transport for the few pressed between curb and
    commerce,
where a child plays in the womb-fed dark
until someone, anyone, brakes for cheap
one-day labor and they climb in,
leaving only dust, to let the journey end.

Visiting Day

for C. and A.

I watch the tulips rise from the ground
like stones from this ashen place
and the bare wires of rose, shining thin,
thorns for the days that drift
to years, each green spike
spent on this March, March morning.

Snow broke my sleep at dawn.
And now the prison barbs
coiled in the ice—who will touch them?
or say "We are the men who dare
to crawl home from this place." My friend wants
to sleep outside—the cold cannot

change his mind. His face, softened now
by a woman—spare and loving.
Like others here, they retreat to touch
in this blue, smoky room. The guards pace
like ratchets in a clock. "Campers," they cry out.
Four men rise from the couch
like denim clouds

who must return—as we all must
to our caged rooms—to sleep with fire
even as snow pools white
on the concrete sky.

Trash Run

He hopped a gray prison truck
to the Flint Drive Dump Site,
freedom on a flatbed,
wedged between leaf and carton
for moments unending until
the hydraulic arm lifted,
shot debris to bedsprings
and bicycles bent from hauling.

There in the cool of Carson's refuse
he lay still as rock. The guard
closed in, clicked fingers, and the bed
fell. Dual tires rolled back and forth,
each bag collapsed in a pop
and his eyes, the salty moons
that never rose to ride the road again.

Later that day, the count cleared
save one. They fumbled through archives
to unearth his picture, the sum of years
broken in slow desperate motion.
No time will tell who fed the throttle,
who ordered the tires to roll
the field of Caterpillars and paper.

The Somali Cab Driver Tells
of Ethnic Cleansing:
Hart Senate Building, Washington, D.C.

He drives in the mirror:

"You a lawyer or a lobbyist?"

No. I work alone.

"You want something?"

Yeah, what about you?

"When I came to this country
I worked in the Somali Embassy.
They began thinning the population.
They knew where to find me."

You started driving a cab?

"Four hard years. I go to Howard.
The best black college in the country.
It's bad out there but I can do it.
We are fifteen—family in the Sudan,
Toronto, and America."

And if you leave?

"In Africa there are 53 to 54 countries—
three are democratic. The rest
kill what they do not like."

You better let me out here.

And the black heart of Africa
is dying in D.C. cabbies
fallen from their home.

At the River's Edge

Montgomery, Alabama

Down here at the confluence of the Coosa
and Talapoosa, the Alabama winds brown
through the red clay of this southern city,
you can fairly smell the blood wedged in the banks
of this great river spilling its way to Mobile.

Today, James Meredith joined hands with Jesse
    Helms
to unearth the southern cross and we in the West
look on smugly without a trace of water to defend.
Where now does the river run, with so few
to feel the anguish of its claws? But I stand here,
Alabama, and make words like
bowls to hold you, to hold you in my arms.

And though they will not do, you run through me,
make silt out of my eyes. I come back a log
bloated on your brown belly and float
the three hundred miles to sea, your skies so full
of rain they cry for the bones
that bevel darkness beneath my feet.
Down here where the river runs free and cold to
    the sea.

black english vernacular

found poem from a text on
black speech and its interpretation

he home, we happy
he be late
we be there
they was early

john work yesterday
he work every day
they works downtown
he done his work on time

we ain't got no coffee nowhere

he done lived there for years
he be dead now
he home, we happy

Until They Come Home

for Levi and Rachel

After the police took the Biblical names given you,
scoured arms and backs for clues, we the nameless
    in your wake
knew there were words you will never touch again:
monster, the black headdress he wore
stalking dark the trailer window
who bore small fear in the whole of you,
and now the worm of boyfriend's failed hate
sleeps alone in a crowded cell.

As we drove to the thrift store,
hunger gathered in your mouths like rain
till Levi burst out, *"Milk!"* and held
the cold white to his lips and drank it all.
Then the quick slap of another word: *belt,*
black with silver studs poking from its leather core.
What stories did he bury in the throats of you,
hair curled for a month of Sundays?

Once inside, the two of you rocked the hangers
for pants, dress, sweater, shoes—with no laces for
    her, no—
and a word came: *stun gun.* I held her foot: *"Not if
    I tie them tight,*
he won't do it again." Rachel, you dressed for more
    than church,
purged aisle after aisle till the blue and red skirt

matched all but the most seasoned of surrogate
    shoppers.
The cashier blinked at the familiar scurry
of hands clothed at last.

Outside the sun crested west and we fed again,
small faces who seemed to eat all day. At the
    Carson Plains Market
Friday paychecks dribbled in, but mother, late in a
    lost car,
feared the worst. No doctor, no father,
"Where have you taken my children?" We passed the
    hours
hearing of old homes broken with family stones
and knew no God would rise to still the coyote's
listless cry come from the cold ridge beyond.

When the stubble of Ford finally slowed and she
    poured out,
black hair a snarl of pain and tired worry, kids
    running
screaming, *"Mom, mom!"* I knew there was no
    home,
no safe place that would ever give shelter from the
    desert,
only a trailer floor filled with socks and stories
of how it used to be, before poor, before this new
    man
came wild through the door to make graves
of two so small as you.

Those People

Those people on the street
soiled with the grain of hunger
and thrift store bins, those people
lying next to you on cold red bricks
go to work, break bread, and eat
in the plum stairwell of Reno's dry lights.

Those people dream darkness will slip
from the fingers of their children,
and the shelter will stay open one more night.
Those people, hardened in the rafters
of downtown lines, hand their best smiles
to soup kitchen chefs every morning,
drown hope in foolish talk of California,
bus rides, and relatives that curl with each passing
     day.

Those people lying next to you
wear my shoes, your hat, and no name.
Come, let us breathe the steam table
smoking in their eyes.
If mercy can be shown
let us not forget the place-keepers
addled with keys and coffers,
who collect small dreams from children—
football, cribbage, and rag dolls,

we who deduct those people in food bank ledgers,
and still they blow like ice into our lives.

The Stonecutter

for Ken "The Moth" Meller

A convicted killer was shot and
killed by sheriff's deputies Friday
when they stormed a prison
infirmary where he'd held a female
doctor hostage for ten hours.
— *Reno Gazette-Journal,*
October 14, 1989

Kenneth wrote his first poem
three days ago. His eyes began to thaw.
He was stoned. There were "hints
and wisps and pieces of heart." No one
knew it was "The Last Poem." Now they share
a cinderblock room without him.

Mothman. Was it the bones
of this prison led him to her,
she who freely gave the heart a listen,
two-and-a-half years out of medical school?
He is home now, in an empty place,
and she, torn from the flesh
who came to heal in her hands.

As they braille the hollow of his grave,
now twelve hours gone,
their poems will darken,
but he will ride the voices
who cannot bear naming
as they recede to cells
this black morning of his passing.

Stones break for the seven who sat
as he read and salted the passage
to hell with tears. If there is a God
who can know these horrors
he surely let him go last night,
and released her from that cold,
cold yearning for death
that came so quickly to call.

Bathing in the River of Ashes

> The next time we meet, any of us,
> it will be on the ashes of all that we
> once cherished.
>
> —Henry Miller

Four women wash coffee skin. A *tikka* on the brow.
Children bob in a river of white and brown.
On either side of the gorge, Shiva and Bissnu swim
    in the grass.
The Dying House is white with the plumage of
    robes.
One day, two, it may be a week before the film of
    death
clogs in their cheeks and they are carried to the
    logs,
stacked like stones with millet and barley to burn.
Some take as many as five hours. Two men tend to
    the body
that blazes; five hundred rupees to snap before the
    temple.
The poor and swollen below the bridge. In Nepal
one must lie close to the river of ashes.

Still more children fly from rocks above the river,
    stab the water
and rise in a cackle of joy. Clothes trickle in and
    out of the sweet liquid,
dry on the reeds. The pads rise from the water like
    gray thumbs
and each day the murmur of death descends upon
    their flat faces.

For two thousand years they have waded a river too
    strong for Shiva,
and when it spills into the Ganges, for India. Water
    buffalo surge
its banks, burst forth a snarl of air, ride the
    minerals and mud
to a pool where they seize the last strobe of sun
    from Annapurna.
Cars cloak the streets and buses throttle ashes to
    sky.
No one comes to the river without a careful
    knotting.
Even the dogs listen for the scrawl of water on
    death's distant shore.
Women, thinned with pride, turn the few drops of
    wet into urns and walk
the streets that empty to homes. But always
    they go,
laughing with children in a wrinkle of quiet feet.

Acknowledgments

Grateful acknowledgment is made to the following publications, in which some of these poems originally appeared: "Nevada No Longer," in *The Comstock Quarterly* (1989); "Hawthorne," in *neon* (1994); "Tumbleweeds and Toenails: Weed Abatement in Silver Springs," in *Halcyon* (1996); "Magpie Funeral," in *Writers' Forum* (1994); "They Go Gathering Pine Nuts," in *Nevada Weekly* (1995); "A Brown Man in the Kitchen" (Spanish and English), in *Calapooya Collage 18* (1994); "Madonna in Traffic," in *TumbleWords: Writers Reading the West,* edited by William L. Fox (Reno: University of Nevada Press, 1995); "Visiting Day," in *A Lustrum* (1995); "At the River's Edge" and "The Stonecutter," in *Calapooya Collage 15* (1991); "Those People," in *Grain* (1992).

Many thanks to the Sierra Arts Foundation for a Professional Artist's Grant, awarded in 1995, which helped me to complete this book.

Finally, were it not for the careful reading of this manuscript by Roseanne Olds, it simply would be incomplete today. I thank her as a poet must thank an audience: for listening, for wondering, and for each hint of suggestion that came slowly from her eyes. She has made her thoughtful presence known.